1

~

Dedication

to the
many astonishing animals
and
wondrous places of our lives.

~

GoosemusiC Publishing Inc.
Sharon, Connecticut 06069

Goosemusicstories@gmail.com

Published May 1, 2014

1st edition

Talking For Animals

An Inspirational Journey

by

Roger Ethier

Copyrighted May, 2014

I know nothing else but miracles...
To me every hour of the light and dark is a miracle,
Every cubic inch of space is a miracle,
Every square yard of the surface of the earth is
spread with miracles.
Every foot of the interior swarms with miracles.

Walt Whitman

Index

Author's Prologue

Part 1

Animal Relationships

Part 2

Human Relationships

Part 3

Animal Tragedies

Author's Prologue

There is a mystical place that I call my secret home and where I have taken my animal friends since early childhood. Although many of the have long since passed memories of all of them are still here. The Meadow Lark that I found on that spring morning beside the road after she had been hit by an automobile is here. She fills me with happiness and gratitude as I look at her with her quizzing eyes. Daily she flies from tree limb to tree limb and often stops to sing her melodious songs before setting up her nesting in a nearby field. Other animal friends are here also, all of them that I have written about and many more.

Because I become so alive when I enter my secret home, I am instantly aware of the natural, beautiful and bountiful environment around me and my harmony within it. And when I observe my animal friends I am overwhelmed with a sense of awe and wonder and I know with certainty that the entire universe is coded for harmony, happiness, health and life and that everything is totally connected on an infinite number of levels.

When reading Talking for Animals I invite you to enter into my secret home while creating your own special place within yourself and together we will take an inspirational journey and observe the awe and wonder of our mystical animal friends, and our relationships to them and the magical Planet Earth.

Part 1

Animal Relationships

Love animals. God has given them the rudiments of thought and joy untroubled.

Do not trouble their joy, don't harass them, don't deprive them of their happiness, don't work against God's intent.

Man, do not pride yourself on superiority to animals, they are without sin, and you, with your greatness, defile the earth with your appearance on it, and leave the traces of your foulness after you---

Alas, it is true of almost every one of us!

Fyodor Dostoyevsky

Talking For Animals

An Inspirational Journey

1.

Gift of Life

"Guard the house," I tell my pint-sized Westy Terrier as I grab my hat and begin my daily jog along the Potomac River. The Westy moves from the doorway to the kitchen, where she is enticed to "sit-up" up with a "yum," and she hangs around as long as there is someone there. When alone, Lacy McGee will lie on a rug next to the door "protecting the house," or more than likely she will head for a large sofa or a soft bed.

Outside, I pause for a moment to watch a scarlet Cardinal, one of three on my property, and a group of yellow finches at a feeder. They no longer fly away when I pass-by but seem to understand that I mean no harm, and merely shuffle and continue their feeding frenzy. In the trees, three squirrels are busy carrying tufts of branches and leaves to reinforce their nests against the winds and the heavy rains. They, too, will use my feeders during the winter when food is more difficult to collect. For both, the birds and squirrels and in fact most of wildlife every minute of every day is a battle for survival; to eat, to escape predators and to protect their habitat.

As I begin my leisurely run along the Potomac a beaver slips into the water leaving only a silent ripple and I see a dark shadow with the large, undulating, flat tail and webbed feet swimming easily below the surface. The beaver enters his lodge from below the surface of the water and disappears, and I quietly affirm to myself that beyond all doubt animals are separate and independent, a priceless part of our vibrant living world and recall words committed to memory years ago, words I knew instinctively were true, even as a youngster.

They are not brethren, they are not underlings; they are other nations, caught with ourselves in the net of time and life, fellow prisoners of the splendor and travail of earth.

Often I choose a longer route to my office, a remote pathway that circles away from the Potomac into open country and here I often see in the winter tracks printed upon a blanket of fresh snow crossing my pathway. They are the narrow tracks of a fox, small round paws with a claw in the front and with the rear paws placed perfectly on top of the front prints. I followed them once and inside of the woods the tracks joined with another fox, and I vividly pictured the two beautiful red foxes flashing large, silken tails, one beside the other like a matched team of proud workhorses trotting under trees, and out into open fields. At one point the tracks of one fox shot off in long, galloping strides across a small field and then circled back, still with galloping strides and attacked the other fox. Over and over they wrestled and romped while disrupting the snow inside of a wide circle. The pair then continued on as if nothing had happened, prancing one beside the other and painting four soft, mystical lines through a distant field that appeared to lead into the infinity of the silver horizon. Although I felt that I was invading their innocent privacy, I continued to follow the tracks deep into woods. Under the darkness of a large white pine tree with long branches nearly touching the ground I found two small pockets burrowed into the pine needles where both foxes had rested, one beside the other while keeping each other warm before they continued on their mystical journey.

2.

Mystical Talk

We form mutual pacts with animal kingdoms and although we do not share a common verbal language we are able to communicate. Perhaps animals recognize the sounds of our voices or simply observe our body language. Possibly, they merely watch our actions or even understand our words and sentences. And the reverse is also true, that animals transmit body language to us, and we simply watch what they do, which we may or may not recognize nor perceive correctly. However, there also appears to be at least one other level of communication, a part of the intricate web of life which is outside of our own practical everyday experience and about which we know little or nothing, yet that seems to be a critical but mysterious part of animal's everyday communications.

~

A nurse who works in Emergency Care in an Inner City, Chicago Hospital finally relaxes after working many overtime hours with a team providing emergency surgery to victims of violence-driven injuries. At her home in a suburb just outside of Chicago, her companion a small dog anticipates her arrival. A camera records the precise moment that she leaves the Emergency Unit to return home from miles away on her unscheduled and long overdue journey. At that same moment, the dog mysteriously awakens and runs to the door and excitedly waits for her to return.

~

In the flat bush country of Kenya a camera records an elephant passing her trunk over her dead mate for a very long time, gently touching his skin as if communicating, or perhaps as part of a self-healing or an understanding process.

Nearby and later in the day, another young elephant from the same herd stops at dried bones lying near a watering pond. The elephant lifts the bones and caresses them with her trunk. A wildlife park ranger who is watching tells a friend who is also viewing the encounter that the bones were those of her mother who died here three years before, shortly after the baby was born.

~

A gorilla in captivity in a zoo in California lapses into a state of severe depression when her baby dies. A human friend is able to communicate to her without words that she has another baby for her, and the gorilla becomes excited. When she is given the new baby, a kitten, she recovers from her depression and cares for it as if her own. Her body movements and deep penetrating eyes communicate her heartfelt gratitude.

~

Thousands of similar recorded examples exist of silent communications among animals and between us and animals. Joy Adamson in *Born Free* and Diane Fossey in *Gorillas in the Midst* are the soul searing images of dedication, love, emotion, compassion and commitment to communities of animals without human verbal communication. Yet, while living on the animals terms, and within their habitats, the researcher's days are packed full with communications, silent or boisterous, and with intense, impassioned emotions and feelings between the hosts and the guests.

3.

Interrupted Lives

Animals always wear their emotions on their sleeves; a puppy's unrestrained love, a bird's cheerful song, a gorilla's deep and sensitive feelings, a cat's stoic independence, a goose's uncompromising fidelity, family and social life, a moose's and a bear's ferocious protection toward their mates and siblings, and an eagle's uncompromising grace, freedom and splendor. Like innocent children, animals openly show their emotions and feelings as they clearly demonstrate a special relationship of harmony and understanding which is spread across all living kingdoms, between animals and other animals, between animals and their habitat, and between animals and humans.

~

A large flock of Canada Geese always stopped to rest and feed at our New England Homestead in Northern Massachusetts during their Spring and Fall migrations each year. The farm is west of the Great North – South Flyway, the normal migration route for Canada Geese transiting that region. However each year they detoured inland to stop at the farm, the same small farm on which six geese of the flock were born and from which the flock originated. These six had led the flock to the farm for a respite during their semi-annual 2000 mile migrations.

As an elderly woman, my mother watches, 500 geese land in her field and the wild migrating Canada Geese recognize her. They hardly shuffle as they make a path for her when she walks among them scattering corn. She talks to them and calls them by their names, names she gave them years before when they were still goslings. They respond with honking and by eating corn from her hands. The flock of geese remain in her fields nearly a week to rest and feed.

A year after she dies the geese stop at the farm to rest and feed. But they are uncommonly restless when they land, and honk constantly. Together as one flock, one community, they appear to be asking, "Where is she? Where is the Gentlewoman? Can you tell us where she has gone?"

~

Along a major, busy highway in Virginia near Dulles Airport as I watch while parked beside the highway, a sparrow pesters a small box turtle by loudly and excitedly chirping, pecking at him, and jumping up and down on his shell when he exits woods, traverses a small carpet of grass, and begins to cross the busy highway. I quickly move my van to block the traffic from hitting the turtle and force the traffic to route around me. The small sparrow continues in a frenzy to alert the turtle. The turtle finally catches on and reluctantly turns around and returns back to the protective grass and the woods, out of the danger of speeding automobiles, led by the sparrow that finally quiets down as soon as the turtle leaves the busy highway and enters the woods.

~

While working on a project on a sheep farm in Madras Oregon a story is told of a Mountain Dog that the farmer had purchased in the Tibetan Highlands. "This is a very special breed of dog," he begins. "He loves sheep. Before the dog came here we lost 30 sheep each year to predators. These sheep at market value are worth over $1,000 apiece but since he came here two years ago we have lost only one sheep to predators. That was during the first year that he was here at the farm. On that one day he was at the Veterinarian's Hospital for an operation to remove porcupine quills his mouth," he says. "He is devoted to the sheep, circles both of the flocks all day, brings them home at night, and sleeps with them. He even licks their young and cares for them as if they were his own."

~

An older, retired couple who are avid conservationists and gardeners live in Northern Virginia just outside Washington, DC. Their home is located in a beautiful wooded area and they are thrilled with their many quiet encounters with wildlife. "One day," Eli quietly begins, "before dawn in early winter we spied a red fox that was quietly and quickly covering our large yard looking for food. He was a beautiful creature who, after making his rounds simply disappeared into a ten acre wooded lot across the street. Each day he would reappear at the same time and continue the same ritual. In the Spring he returned with three offspring and his mate. They were beautiful animals, so precise with each step, and so filled with awareness."

The couple was awed with a sense of wonder by the beauty of the foxes, the grace of the mystical movements and by the mere presence of the red foxes near them. However, when houses are built across the street with no provisions for the foxes or other wildlife, the foxes no longer show up at dawn and the couple feels a deep and sad loss of kinship with their natural world and the foxes, a feeling that persists even today, ten years later.

~

`   One Spring day at a small farm near my childhood homestead in New England a neighbor discovered a baby squirrel on the ground that had fallen from its nest. She carried him to my folks who cared for him. They fed him from a baby's milk bottle and named him Peter.

Throughout the ensuing years he roamed free outside all day, and dad built a beautiful, two story squirrel house where he slept at night. Many years later and a week after dad died the squirrel too died, and mom told my young son, "I think that Peter the squirrel died of loneliness, the loneliness of missing Gramps." And the boy knew instinctively that what his grandmother said was true.

4.

Moving Rainbows

Consider that animals within many ancient and modern cultures in both the West and the East are perceived with awe and wonder, and as spiritual thoughts sent to permanently fill a special need or niche, perhaps even like angels. Such perceptions dismantle simplistic explanations, and contradict scientific rationalizations for destroying animals and their habitats which are grounded in narrow mechanized science, religious traditions, naked habits, greed and profits. In fact, stepping back for an honest, perceptive glance beyond ourselves into our vibrant, living universe reinvigorates our instinctive thoughts and conclusions and leads to our own intrinsic wisdom, a crystal clear understanding, and an absolute confidence in our own self-worth and the intrinsic worth all living beings and this living planet.

~

At our rural New England farm, my folks accepted without question unwanted, dogs, puppies, cats and kittens. Many of them were abused or not properly cared for. When the animals were healthy again they were lovingly passed to deserving and caring families for a nominal cost.

At the farm several young puppies of many different sizes and breeds are romping, stomping and playing in an outdoor puppy yard. "They are families," mom tells my nine year old son, her grandson. "They are always happier when they are together. They have emotions, feelings and communicate with each other and with us all the time, and when they are taken back here for a visit, even years later, they become ecstatic and immediately recognize us, this building, and members of their own families."

Later in the day, when the boy carries ten baby, multi-colored parakeets on his fingers and in their innocence they are content to sit on his fingers fluttering their wings, but they do not fly away, she says, "They remind me of small, innocent, beautiful angels." The boy marvels at the astonishing colors and the innocence of the birds and their relationship to his grandmother and to himself. And as he continues to watch them fluttering their colorful wings that look like many multicolor, moving rainbows he realizes that his grandmother's description of the parakeets as small, innocent, beautiful angels describes exactly what he himself feels.

~

As a sailor on "watch" topside a naval ship in a severe nautical storm in the Arctic Ocean, I later chronicle the story of the ship's encounter with breaching whales. "The wind is whipping up large whitecaps and the black sky and churning sea in the distance seem to touch each other. Two hundred yards ahead of us a dozen large, mature humpback whales are breaching. They look like gigantic ghosts and are only visible as dark shadows through the heavy mist and fog as they reach high out of the water to gulp air, one after the other. Sometimes two humpbacks are out of the water at the same time. At the top of their leaps only their tails are submerged.

This is not breaching for survival only, the humpbacks appear to be in competition with each other. Each of them is attempting to leap higher than any other. When they crash back into the turbulence of the rolling waves they continue their downward decent into a deep dive. Near the bottom in one motion they turn their bodies in the opposite direction and accelerate upward vertically at tremendous speeds, finally breaking the surface with one last powerful push.

The entire crew of the ship watched and was completely transfixed by the spectacle. All day and far into the darkness of night this spectacle of breaching and competition continued at intervals, and when we finally sailed away we could hear for miles their tumultuous return to the water that appeared to sound like rolling thunder."

5.

Harmony and Wonderment

All living beings bring to us and this vibrant world astonishing harmony and wonderment. Look closely at a bird's wing, a cat's paw, a hog's snout, a horse's hoof, a tiger's coat, a puppy's face, a butterfly's design and color, and an elephant's trunk and ears. Also, listen to any bird's song, the wolf pack's singing, the dolphin's incessant talk, a horses echoing whinny or a lion's reverberating roar. Observe the delicate art and unique sounds, the infinite precision and the limitless purposes. Watch a loon dive straight down into the water to a depth of over one hundred feet. Silently follow the path of a wild animal that you observed passing-by shortly before, and begin to feel the innate awareness of his senses, and the stealth and the strength of his body and mind. Can even one animal be created in laboratories or by the inventions of humans?

A Native American speaks with innate knowledge and absolute confidence when he says, *"Understanding begins with love and respect. It begins with love of the Great Spirit, and the Great Spirit is the life that is in all things—all creatures and plants and even the rocks and minerals. All things, and I mean all things—have their own will and their own way and their own purpose; this is to be respected. Such a respect is not a fooling around or an attitude only. It is a way of life and means that we never stop realizing to carry out our obligations to ourselves and our environment."*11

~

Beside the road I saw a meadow lark today. She had been hit by a car and lay as if sleeping. When I picked her up, her body was limp but still warm; her eyes were opened and seemed to be looking at me with a quizzing gaze. Only a slight trace of blood on her stomach marred her exquisite colors. She was bright yellow with wing feathers rich chocolate and milk white, and she was about the size of a robin. As I looked at her on this brisk spring day marveling at her beauty I wondered the purpose of the vivid, striking colors so conspicuous in a summer field. I also wondered about her brood and if her brood had already been hatched. If so, could they make it on their own?

I carried her to the nearby field while lightly pressing her to my chest hoping that somehow my heartbeats would awaken her and placed her in a grassy nest in her meadow home. Her beauty was astounding. As I wandered back to the road the deep silence of the meadow seemed to suddenly erupt into a plethora of bird and insect songs. I listened. The clear high pitch song of a meadow lark echoed sweetly above the other sounds in a prolonged mystical poem before it faded into the distance.

6.

Anima Mundi

Among the Ancients, the word "animal" meant "soul." Before the modern theologians narrowed the use of the word "soul" to humans alone, and then sanctified and stamped the narrowed description as an infallible truth, the word was used by the ancient civilizations including scientists to define the soul as unexplainable and mysterious, an intricate web of life which united all of earth's living creatures. Likewise, "anima mundi" was used by the same ancient civilizations to define the one force that united all of nature and through which we are all able to connect.

~

The Caretaker of a Horticulture Center along the Potomac River tells the story of a large black snake to a friend.

"Old George, he lives under the house...has for years. During the winter he crawls in under there and comes out in Spring. Old George and me recognize each other and stay out of the other's way. One hot summer day, I was mowing hay with the tractor up there in front of the main house and went under the large magnolia tree with limbs nearly touching the ground and continued right on.

Old George must have been lying on one of the limbs I shooked, getting his afternoon nap cause when I looked back I saw Old George ... I could tell it was George with the white under his chin and his size, you know... and he was mad and was coming after me right up on his tail. I jumped down from the tractor and run into the house with George right behind me running up on his tail. I slammed the door shut...and heared Old George hit the closed door."

~

Throughout North America, all summer long monarch butterflies fly from one flowering plant to another, accumulating energy they draw from the sweetness of the blossoms. Early one morning in late September as I watch from my wild flower garden in Northern Virginia, one solitary monarch takes off from a large thistle and rises in tight circles high above the trees, and without hesitating flies due south. Later that same morning, hundreds of Monarchs are flying overhead, some solo and others in groups of two or three, all heading south as part of their annual 2000 mile migrations. Also, elephants, lions, cats, horses, geese, ducks, fish, birds, and perhaps all of wildlife have similar migrating abilities.

The unbelievable feats of migration, navigation and homing by the animal kingdoms are not by chance, nor are they automatic or robotic. Accumulated research on a variety of species of birds reveals that a startling volume of information is processed and integrated during migratory flights. Easily more advanced than even the Polynesian Mariners who navigated the Pacific without instruments from one island to the next by observing, analyzing and processing delicate clues available in nature, birds use the same resources available to humans as well as many additional informational aids that are not able to be perceived by humans.

Not only do birds use celestial patterns and recognize wind and sun movements and landmarks similar to the human seafarers of history but they also employ ultraviolet and polarized light, the sense of smell, infra sounds, and the earth's magnetic field..."a whole set of very sophisticated guidance systems," one renowned researcher remarks. "... a whole set of navigational strategies," another says. "(Birds) seem remarkably like people (since) they use a variety of cues in their travels... (and) may even use several cues simultaneously, checking one against the other," a third researcher summarizes. *2

~

Hundreds of miles from land the majestic Wandering Albatross, the master of air currents soars above the breaking waves over open water and will glide over the eddy wind streams of the world several times during the course of one year. One day as I watched from a Naval Ship, a Great Wandering Albatross that was obviously a mature adult male soared above our ship sporting a ten or eleven foot wingspan and flashed brilliant white and black in the sunlight. He then glided into the horizon very low and banked at an angle of 90 degrees so that the tip of one wing barely touched the surface, spraying a white mist. The brilliant black color on the upper sides of the tips of his wings was in full view. All the time I watched him he never flapped his wings but rode on the air currents, and appeared to use his great webbed feet even more than his tail for navigating. He hung around the ship for most of that day soaring into the far horizon and then suddenly reappearing again above the ship like a mystical, airborne ghost.

~

On another voyage while approaching the coast of Italy very high in a clear blue sky a magnificent Frigate Bird, another master of flying was riding upward on the warm columns of air. His wingspan is smaller than the albatross and he has a forked tail. The Frigate Bird remains near land while the Albatross roams the open oceans of the world. The Frigate Bird also has no oil on his feathers and must grab fish with his hooked bill from the surface of the water, or steal them from others, without getting wet.

This bird too was a male, marked by a brilliant red throat pouch that he inflated and deflated. "As agile as a swallow" someone once said of the Frigate Bird that has a body that weighs only three pounds and a wingspan of seven to eight feet.

The Frigate Bird had reason to be there. He was keeping his eye on a nearby flock of sluggish flying Boobies. The Boobies have webbed feet designed for underwater fish catching and have located a school of fish. The agile Frigate Bird is hanging around looking to steal their catch. The Boobies are excellent divers and swimmers, and easily catch fish underwater.

They are diving from altitudes of up to three hundred feet, straight down with wings flapping, and then clasping both wings together just before they hit the surface of the water. They enter the water as straight as an arrow and cut a long underwater arc back to the surface, hardly slowing down, and all the while collecting and swallowing fish.

As soon as they are airborne again the Frigate Bird is "Johnny-on-the-spot" and swoops down on the Boobies and causes them to vomit the fish, which the Frigate Bird catches in midair for a meal of its own. Time and again the patient Frigate Bird waited for the Boobies to surface and to fly into the air before he ambushed then and stole a meal for himself by catching fish in midair that the Boobies had dropped.

Part 11

Human Relationships

*I think that I could turn and live with animals, they
are so placid and self-contained,
I stand and look at them long and long.
They do not sweat and whine about their condition,
They do not lie awake in the dark and weep for their
sins.
They do not make me sick discussing their duty to
God,
Not one is dissatisfied, not one demented with the
mania of owning things,
Not one kneels to another, or to his kind that lived
thousands of years ago,
Not one is respectable or unhappy over the whole
earth.*   Walt Whitman

7.

Jeanne and the Shetlands

Walking along the old split-rail wooden fence back to the old farmhouse Jeanne wonders if she should tell anyone what she has done. Jeanne spends every summer at her grandfather's farm. "One thing I'm sure of, I want to ride the Shetlands again," she says to herself. "And I want to do it alone, the ponies seem calmer and happier and I like being alone with them. If I tell anyone, Gramps, Grams or even Little Jack they will want to go to the field with me, or even stop me from riding at all. That's not a good idea!"

Jeanne is nine. She is short like most kids who are nine, and her auburn hair has bleached out nearly white in the summer sun. Her eyes are gray like her Grandmother's and her skin has turned a healthy dark tan. "She's as wild as an Indian her Grandfather often says."

Jeanne spends every moment she can with her grandfather and her grandmother at their farm.

She loves to run and is nearly as fast as her cousin, Little Jack, who is three years older and who also spends his summer vacations at the farm. At daybreak each morning, Jeanne runs to the old boxcar in the middle of the field where the grain is stored and fills a long wooden trough with oats for the ponies. Three ponies are already waiting when she arrives and after a bit of pushing and shoving the ponies line up and eat the oats from the trough. While the ponies chomp on the oats Jeanne brushes each one of them, singing all the while.

She uses two brushes, one in each hand. First she rubs away the crusty mud and other debris picked up when the ponies rolled over in the fields with a metal Kerry Comb. "Rub-a-bub-rub-bub-bub...," she sings as she scrapes off the dry dirt. "Rub-a-bub-rub-bub-bub."

Then she shines their entire coats with a second brush, a horse brush with long stiff bristles, and she changes the words to "shin-shine-shin-shin-shine", which she sings over and over until the three ponies are completely brushed. "Shin-shine-shin-shin-shine". All the while the ponies continue eating and stand very still, moving only once in a while to chase away a pesky horsefly.

When Jeanne finishes brushing the ponies and they have finished their feed they often trot away to the center of the field, and roll over and over and immediately cover themselves again with mud and grass. "You're doing that on purpose," Jeanne screams at them and laughs, and when the ponies are again on their feet they whinny loudly in total agreement.

The three ponies then gallop full speed across the back fields, their golden tails and manes flying in the wind and their hooves drumming a low thunder, as Jeanne watches. Around and around they gallop three times, until they finally stop in a far corner. Together they rear-up and buck, over and over until finally, each pony settles down and begin to graze the fresh, green grass.

But this morning is different. After the last pony is brushed, Jeanne grabs her mane with one hand and easily swings herself up on her back. She has often thought about riding the ponies, but now she doesn't even think, she just does it, automatically.

The fields are out of the sight of everyone, lucky for Jeanne. An apple orchard runs all along the back fence and the two other sides of the fields are bordered by woods and the barn. On the fourth side is her grandparents farm house, but it is far away and separated by a high knoll and two large fields. During the winter when there is no feed in the fields the ponies eat hay inside the barn. But no sooner has the snow disappeared than the tender grass shoots spring up and covers the ground, and soon the ponies are outside roaming the fields. All day long the ponies chomp away at the grass in the back fields, and only stop at night to sleep. In the morning Jeanne is back feeding them oats and brushing them again, before the ponies continue their ritual of galloping three times around the field before settling down in the pasture and chomping the grass.

Jeanne has just finished brushing the third and last pony when suddenly she is on the back of one of the Shetlands flying through the fields with the cool fresh wind whipping through her hair. She can hardly feel the pony beneath her as she holds its mane very firmly with both hands, her knees tight against the pony's ribs. Instinctively, she leans forward into the wind so that her head is nearly level with the pony's head. On her left the other two ponies are racing beside her taking long strides in an effort to keep up, and she can hear the low rumble of their hooves. *Galump...galump... galump...galump...galump.*

When they reach near the end of the field and the fence, the ponies don't even slow down but continue galloping and turn sharply right very close-by the fence. Jeanne automatically loosens her right hand from the pony's mane and uses it to help balance herself as she leans into the sharp turn. She hardly hears herself yelling in unison with the beats of their hooves, "Yi-pee, Yi-pee, Yi-pee, Yi-pee, Yi-pee."

They gallop around the fields three times, with all three of the ponies racing each other, and the small girl, Jeanne, crouching low on the back of the outside pony, holding tight with her fingers to the flying, golden mane. Finally, the ponies tire and stop. Jeanne slides to the ground, and quickly steps away, just before the ponies start their daily ritual of rolling in the grass, bucking and rearing-up in the air, as they always do before they settle down and begin to eat the grass.

The earth feels like balloons beneath Jeanne's feet at first, and even when she finally walks back to the old farmhouse she still feels like she is walking on soft air. But she doesn't tell anyone that she has taken her first ride on a pony, not Grams, not Gramps or not even Little Jack. And each morning from then on, if she is alone with the ponies in the field, after she feeds them she chooses one pony, a different one each day and swings herself easily onto the pony's back and rides like the wind racing with the other two ponies until the ponies tire and stop. Jeanne then quickly slides back to the ground and steps away, just before the ponies start their daily ritual of rolling, bucking, rearing up, and whinnying loudly

8.

Please take Care of Her

A Ferrier who travels throughout central Massachusetts and Southern New Hampshire to shoe horses also owns a small farm in central New England, where he cares for animals that are old and no longer wanted.

"They are retired, like humans," he says, as he quietly and gladly funds his project from his own pocket not telling anyone, contented with daily contact and relationships with all of them. He has four donkeys, one horse, four ponies, twenty seven geese, five dogs, a crippled raven, a small flock of bantam chickens and ducks, a canary, three finches, a pair of peach faced love birds and a parrot.

Sadie a miniature donkey, Goldie a Shetland, the horse and the geese are all over forty years old. The raven, Joe is over fifty, and Fritz a long hair dachshund is twenty. When one of the ponies becomes totally blind the horse assumes the role of her protector and she accepts. He leads the pony around the fields and back into the barn each evening, not allowing other animals to taunt or bully her. They become inseparable.

"Why shouldn't animals retire and have peace in their later years, the man asks. "Must they be killed just because we have no need for them, like milk cows, laying hens, some race horses and riding horses, ponies, greyhounds and many pets are treated today? Fifty thousand racing greyhounds are destroyed each year in the US simply because they are no longer so-called *first place achievers.*

Point to a unique, small, astonishing animal and the first question we ask is, What good is it? When wildlife is seen in the woods by someone with a gun it gets shot," he concludes.

A sense of community with our living world and understanding the tranquility, honesty and uniqueness that all animals bring to our lives unshackles us from these traditional chains of blindness, greed, human domination, and thoughtless cruelty.

~

One summer day a circus pulls into a nearby New England town and a very old man named Benny who has traveled with the circus for fifty odd years brings his Rhesus Monkey to our small farm. "Please take care of her," he pleads to dad. He himself is too frail to care for her any longer. "Her name is Trudy, and I have heard how you care for all animals here," he says. He asks no money. "How do you sell a friend?" he mutters in a hopeless, questioning tone as he lifts his arms in front of him with his hands palms up. He then holds both monkey's hands for a long moment and gently touches her face, one last time. When Benny turns and walks back down the old dirt road he is quietly weeping and Trudy too has tears in her eyes as she continues to stare after Benny long after he is out of sight.

Later in that same year at Christmas time dad explains to his grandson, Little Jack how he cares for the monkey, Trudy.

"When we care for them, in fact when we care for all animals we accept the responsibility for them completely, for their feed and whatever else they need including exercise and companionship. They have no one else to help them when they are confined and cannot help themselves. As he speaks, Trudy, the monkey stares first at him for as long as he speaks, and then at the grandson when he asks questions. Suddenly, she jumps to the floor from the farmer's shoulder and quickly runs behind him. The boy doesn't know what to do or expect so he freezes perfectly still and doesn't even dare to breath or to turn around. Trudy jumps up on his shoulder from behind and then hops back to the farmer's shoulder, as quick as a flash. In her hand is the boy's new Christmas wallet, a gift from his grandparents.

"She is a born pickpocket," dad laughs.

"I didn't feel anything; I had no idea that she was taking my wallet out of my pocket," the boy replies as he places his hand into the now empty back pocket of his new Christmas jeans.

9.

Living Mysteries

Laboratory scientists say that animals cannot shed tears, that they do not have feelings like humans. Perhaps, in the laboratory where animal lives are sterile, dull, and filled with depression and terror, sometimes for as long as forty years for some poor monkeys, perhaps here it appears so. But ask the scientist who observes animals in their wild habitat daily, and who studies their relationships with their families and other animals, who quickly becomes convinced that animals have feelings, emotions and communicate with each other and with us all the time, and to an extent possibly even greater than we communicate with each other.

~

Deep inside of Africa two scientists observe two female giraffes within their natural habitat circle an older male who becomes crippled and is not able to walk any longer. After the females finally and reluctantly leave to join the protective herd, the older male sits down and sheds large, flowing tears of loneliness and helplessness.

~

In California, Dr. Francine "Penny" Patterson, an impressive person in a line of modern day enlightened men and women who are attempting to understanding animal's language confirmed time and again throughout a nearly twenty years study that gorillas have deep personal emotions and feelings which are very similar to our own and communicate with us, their own families and other animals all the time, also in a way similar to our own.

She assisted Koko, a gorilla, to master a language of over 500 words through sign language. Over the years Koko communicated experiences with no prompting from Penny, of what she wanted for her birthday, a name she had given to her young friend a kitten, expressions of approval and disapproval, sadness, happiness and thoughts of what happens when gorillas die. When her friend, Ali Ball, a kitten ran into the road and was accidentally killed by a car Koko at first was silent, but then cried with high pitched sobbing which continued intermittently for a week, and whenever cats were mentioned.

Like humans, animals openly communicate with us and with one another in a world much older than our own and constantly remind us of our frailty, limitations and our dependence on all other living beings and this universal habitat. Ask a trainer of any animal who uses benevolence rather than brute-force, ask him if animals readily communicate with each other and with humans? Question him as to whether or not animals have emotions and feelings akin to our own.

~

Monty Roberts, a Californian who even as a boy was innately drawn to horses and while still a teenager constantly observed wild mustangs through binoculars communicating with each other. Just as with many other sages in other fields, he seemed always to be in harmony with himself and horses when in the presence of horses. While observing the wild mustangs through binoculars he noted subtle communications within the herd and then he honed his knowledge to become one of the greatest horse trainers in the world, listening to and watching horses and deer with benevolence and understanding, and then benevolently and silently asking horses for their cooperation.

Ask this man who has trained thousands of green and remedial horses throughout the world, many in less than thirty minutes by knowing their habits and by watching their body language, and who responded in kind by using his own body language and asking rather than demanding. Ask him if animals are willing to communicate.

Queen Elizabeth of England a horse lover whose family and history of understanding and companionship with horses dates back for centuries, after reading about Monty Roberts' training methods, invited him to England for a demonstration and to talk to him, and she ended up establishing a training center which teaches his training techniques throughout the whole of England. Later the Germans asked him to conduct demonstrations and then also adopted his techniques throughout the country.

"The greatest friend that equines ever had," a friend says. "The very best horse trainer in the world, a man who reads horses, and inspires trust (of humans) in them," another confirms. *18

In fact, Monty Roberts is another one of an enlightened breed of men and women in Western Civilizations who are making the conscious effort to listen, to learn, and to understand how animals communicate with each other and with us, and how we can respond to them.

Compare these enlightened techniques with the horrible beatings used to break the innate wills of animals, and the unmitigated terror and cruelty to many species of wildlife during the so called breaking process by humans today. Elephants, tigers, lions, bears, horses and in fact most all of wildlife are often painfully constrained, beaten and terrified into submission in order to submit to the will of humans. Watch a so-called breaking session of a wild elephant and listen to the screams of pain and terror that resound on and on, throughout the long days and into the nights.

~

Dr. Theodore X. Barber who, after a thirty year career as a behavioral scientist, when he redirected his studies to animal intelligence was astounded and shocked at avian intelligence and the degree that avian thought process is similar to humans. He concludes in his book, "The Human Nature of Birds, A Scientific Discovery with Startling Implications," after six years of research about Avian Intelligence that "birds are not only intelligent, aware and willful; they also can communicate meaningfully with humans and relate to them as close, caring friends."*2

10.

Inspirational Spirits

Animals are our companions and our work mates, our guards, our guardians, and our soul mates. Animals and children in particular are natural soul mates often displaying innocent, respectful and natural bonds with each other. The expediency of destroying an animal or a tree because it is simply a human challenge or the easiest path doesn't exist in a child's world. Children simply don't live there, until we teach them human domination over the rest of the living world, while at the same time tutoring them to ignore the principles of *Reverence for Life* and *The Greater Must Always Protect the Lesser.*

~

A ten year old girl, Inona, is abandoned within the Inner City of New York and comes to the wilderness of the Bayou Country to live with her grandmother. She learns to love, respect and embrace all wildlife and habitat as if they were her own. She gladly spends hour after hour outdoors appreciating the magnificent world of nature. Often she walks to nearby wetlands and sits and watches a White Heron. He is a splendid, proud creature that often prances close-by her before he flies from tree to tree gathering berries and insects.

When she is befriended by a hunter who is looking for a very rare White Heron to add to his lifeless mounted collection of birds, a heron that she often watches, she becomes silent, refusing to tell and feigning ignorance despite the promise of a large sum of money that her grandmother desperately needs. She cannot even begin to fathom the killing of a beautiful creature of the wild for money. Instead, she consciously sides with wildlife, choosing the proud, wild bird over the predator man.

~

A friend is asked to kill a snake that is lying asleep next to her front door. Her boy, a five year old screams loudly and objects at the thought of killing the snake. The friend quietly assures the boy that he would only relocate the snake to nearby woods.

With the boy and his mom accompanying the friend in the early morning chill, the lethargic small black snake is lifted by the tail into a bucket and relocated in woods near the river. Two years later, the boy still waves and laughs when the friend passes by. When he stops to chat, the boy is animated and talks incessantly about the beautiful, baby snake. A special and compassionate bond has developed between the boy and wildlife, and the boy and his mother's friend.

~

Observe closely a herd of cows. Look carefully and see that each one is different in manners, looks and disposition from any other. One is timid, another friendly, a number of them seem to resemble deer or antelope. Others have expressions of vulnerability and femininity. Some jump a fence as gracefully as a gazelle; others are content to graze with the herd. The "boss" is always in the lead or somewhere near the middle but not a bully, although her word is law and the rest of the herd follows her.

When I was a teenager growing up on our small farm, I owned a small, beautiful Guernsey heifer. In the fields she followed me like a puppy, wherever I went. Before school I looked forward to feeding her grain, brushing her, and leading her to pasture. In the evenings she patiently waited for me as I opened the gate, and she followed me into the barn where I fed her grain and lovingly brushed her again. Later, after she freshened, I milked her. Her milk was frothy and fragrant, and after it cooled a two inch thick layer of heavy, golden cream formed, and covered the sweet, honeyed liquid. Today, fifty years later I still remember her silken, light chocolate coat, her thoughtful stare at me, her sweet disposition, and her rich, creamy milk.

~

As a seven year old, while walking along a gravel road near our farm one Spring day I discovered three baby, orphaned skunks. The mother had been hit and killed by a car. They were lying beside their mother in the gutter waiting for her to awaken. I gathered them up, put them inside my shirt and took them home. During the first days mom and I fed them warmed milk from a baby bottle with a rubber nipple. As they get older I fed them cat food in a small dish.

During those first days they often stomped their little paws on the ground as an instinctive warning and raised their tails over their backs, and attempted to spray me. But because of their young ages they were unable to spray. Within a few days however we became friends. Mom called them innocent little angels and we named them

Dandelion, Sweet Pea and Indian Paint which were names of three common wild flowers in our fields.

When they were three months old I took them outside into the fields during the day and watched as they hunted bugs, field mice and ate plant roots. Later I helped to build a shelter for them by modifying a large, open wooden box and cutting a small entrance on one side and placing the box near our garden upside down.

All summer long, the young skunks hunted bugs from tomato, potato, corn, spinach, lettuce and pepper plants. That year the entire garden was bug-free and we produced a very large crop of beautiful vegetables. In the fall all three of my friends left the field and entered nearby woods. I rarely saw them after that although from time to time I saw one of them in the field or crossing the gravel road.

11.

The Newfoundlands

Animals are natural protectors and companions of our children and other loved ones, often intentionally standing between them and possible danger. The beautiful and amazing Newfoundland dogs are legendary for their uncompromising bonds to humans as baby-sitters, lifeguards, ship dogs, draft animals, pack carriers, natural retrievers, protectors and companions.

It's not coincidental that in the original Peter Pan, Nana a Newfoundland was the family baby-sitter, companion, and protector, or that a Newfoundland saved French Emperor Napoleon from drowning, or that on nearly every ship throughout the world during the sailing era there was a Newfoundland, a "Ship's Dog" to carry the painter to shore during danger of shipwrecks and to rescue sailors, or that two Newfoundlands were required life savers on all beaches along the New England Coast in the 19th century. "Touched by Gods of Olympus," it's been said of Newfoundlands. "Spiritual thoughts, passed to us to help us learn, like angels," one eminent and humble lady from New England said when she spoke of all animals.

Our Newfoundlands

Heavy snow storms in January were common in Northern Massachusetts in the early part of the last century, and the weather forecasting was marginal. A pair of fully grown Newfoundland dogs that had grown up with us on our farm always accompanied us the two miles as we walked to school each day. The dogs would then trot back to our small farm and return to the school in late afternoon to accompany us home. Often we tromped through foot deep snow or got caught in a snow storm but we always knew with absolute certainty that we were safe when the Newfoundlands were with us.

One day my two brothers and I, together with the Newfoundlands left our farm for school in early morning just as snow started to fly. Jon was eight and Gene was fourteen. I was ten years old.
By noontime the snow was nearly a foot deep and the wind and snow continued to increase in intensity.

Dad was away, out of town at work and mom was at the farm with no transportation or driving skills. Mom simply told the two Newfoundlands at noontime to "go to the school and get Jon, Gene and Roger." The dogs obediently trotted off and returned to the school and found us waiting for them. Together, we all then headed back to our small farm in foot deep snow holding hands, and with the larger Newfoundland, Skipper gently grasping the wrist of Jon, the smallest of us while trotting beside him. When Jon tired or slipped we simply stopped to rest while Skipper continued to hold onto Jon's wrist and gently to help him to his feet. We then continued our journey unafraid while constantly chatting with each other, content and comfortable knowing with absolute certainty that the Newfoundlands would lead us safely home despite the snow storm.

Less than an hour from the time we left the school building, mom watched us cheerfully climbing the hill to our farmhouse dressed in heavy winter cloths that she had made which were partially covered with snow, while we chatted, threw snowballs and laughed with the affable Newfoundland dogs trotting beside us.

I remember that she prepared a hardy dinner for us that afternoon of home-canned vegetables from our own garden, thickened chicken soup and roast beef all raised on our farm, and topped off with bread pudding with raisons from bread she kneaded the night before and had baked that morning. Meanwhile the Newfoundlands who prefer the outside and cold, snowy weather to the indoors ate their dinners on the porch and then had burrowed under the deep snow and were happily sleeping outside the kitchen door under the snow, one beside the other.

Even when sleeping, Skipper and Smokey always seemed to have smiles on their faces. They really seemed to enjoy every minute of every day. No matter what happened, it didn't matter, nothing seem to bother them.

One time the Newfoundlands seemed to laugh riotously at us although my older brother, Gene and I did anything but laugh. We were scared to death, and stayed in partial shock for weeks.

It was Thanksgiving day. Every Thanksgiving our family always came together for dinner. It was a ritual with most farm families in New England. After one Thanksgiving Dinner while we were all still at the table dad was summing up the harvest at the farm. "The apples and the cider are in the storage house; the potatoes are limed and are in the cellar together with the canned tomatoes, the summer squash, and the piccalilli. The beef and pork are slaughtered, cut-up and wrapped and are in the freezer. On balance, it was a good year."

I was half listening to dad and half watching through a large picture window the pair of Newfoundlands running across the field toward to our farmhouse. Skipper was carrying something very large in his mouth, high above the ground, in a proud, prancing manner. Quietly I excused myself and I slipped out the side door, just behind Gene my older brother who also had been watching the dogs running across the field.

Both of us thought that Skipper was carrying a small dog in his mouth. Perhaps, a dog had been hit by a car and Skipper had picked it up off the street and was carrying it home to be taken care of. But when the pair came closer we realized that it was not a small dog but something larger with no hair and a lot of skin. Both dogs stopped at the edge of the field and were now prancing around in circles, occasionally rearing up on two hind legs and throwing their heads back and forth, much like a couple of young stallions having a great time and really feeling their oats.

Both Gene and I raced across the yard, intercepted Skipper's circle on the second try, and I reached up and grabbed his collar to keep him still and to see what was in his mouth. As soon as I touched his collar, old dutiful Skipper stopped prancing and rearing, and then for the first time we saw the fully cooked turkey.

Would you believe it? Skipper, our dog was prancing around our yard with a fully cooked turkey in his mouth that he most likely picked off the sill of a nearby farmhouse where the lady of the house had placed it to cool. The bird was so large that we couldn't even see any part of the dog's head, but only the turkey, all brown and dripping stuffing from two holes where the neck and wing had once been. With so large a bird, the cook had obviously taken special pains with its preparation; probably working all of the prior day to prepare it and all night to cook it, before taking it from the oven about an hour before the meal and placing it on an outside window sill to cool. But it wouldn't be there, vanished without a trace, like a cloud or a puff of smoke, leaving only the dish or maybe a spot of grease on the window sill.

I was only ten and Gene was fourteen. We both looked across the field half expecting to see a legion of men, women, and children running toward us at full speed, led by a screaming, and partially crazed woman with a long apron and a very large carving knife or cleaver. The cops would be near also, probably with loaded and drawn revolvers and shotguns aiming them at our two dogs. However, there was no one in the field or anywhere in site, at least not yet.

Gene and I dragged Skipper into the barn by his collar and locked both dogs in one of the stalls together with the turkey. Just before we closed the barn door I looked back and stared for a moment at both of the dogs who were lying down and staring back at us with an exceptionally large grin. We closed the door and placed a heavy wooden plank across it, on the outside, a plank that we used to use to keep horses from kicking down the doors in a fit of panic and escaping. Then we padlocked the door with a huge cast iron padlock that had been salvaged from the railroad and been used to temporarily fasten freight cars to the siding while awaiting the arrival of the lead engine.

When Gene and I slipped back inside of the house we again glanced across the field but there was still no one there. In the evening we went back to the stables and only the carcass of the turkey was left, plus half a drumstick. Both dogs were lying there with bloated stomachs, hardly able to acknowledge our presence with a single flop of their fat, lazy tails and with those same wily smiles that seemed to be frozen on their faces. Gene and I buried the carcass and the extra drumstick in the next stall, three feet down and kept the dogs locked in the barn the rest of the week. We never found out where the turkey came from or who it belonged to, nor did my brother and I ever try.

12.

Miracle Workers

In rural New York, another one of an emerging number of visionaries that understand the vital harmony and happiness that animals bring to our lives pursues a personal dream to reform nursing care for our elderly by upgrading the quality of life in nursing homes, and ending loneliness, helplessness and boredom. He calls his project "The Eden Alternative," and uses lush mini-arboretums, a collection of animals, and children to involve elderly residents to pursue a full, happy life. In the "Eden" home, there are three dogs, five cats and more than one hundred birds. Immediately after introduction of animals and plants, allergies, infection rates, and medication rates drop, and the constant noise of conversation and laughter are heard in all the halls.

"Animals, plants and in fact all of life are spiritual thoughts sent to fulfill a special need," one doctor candidly remarks when walking through the new elderly's home.

Indeed! All living beings are interconnected by the web of life and cutting any fiber in that web diminishes the vital harmony in the lives of all of us, including our beloved elderly.

~

A mother of four young children who live close-by my home in Northern Virginia tells me the story of a Sheltie dog continuously circling her children, herding them away from their play yard into a solid group which he could better protect. "On and on he barked, until finally I barely notice that blending in with the shadows on a large sugar maple limb lay a massive black snake resting in the shade of the leaves," she says. The dog had sensed danger to the children and used its natural instincts of rounding up sheep to protect the children.

~

A teenager with epilepsy is warned before each of her unpredictable seizures by her dog. She herself has no warning of the impending seizure. The dog mysteriously rests his paws and his head on her lap to alert her, and then as the seizure takes place he prevents the semi-conscious child from hurting herself by placing his paws on the girl's chest. "A sixth sense that humans don't have," one doctor says when attempting to explain the actions of the dog. "Her loving guardian angel," a nurse quietly whispers.

13.

A Common Soul

Humans and animals share a common, golden, sacred thread, the thread of life. Throughout our passages of life, oxygen and other substances are absorbed into our bodies and then are exhausted as energy and other end products, until the last breath uses an amount of energy that falls below the level of consumption. Then the candle flickers and expires, and finally the thread is broken. In between, the life of every living being, animals, humans and in fact the entire living world explodes with communications, feelings and emotions and glows as a brilliant candle affecting everything and everyone within contact.

A minister in Vermont openly examines our relationships to animals and poses the question: "Do Animals Have Souls?" Later in his published and thought-provoking book "The Souls of Animals" Gary Kowalski openly asks ten questions and proceeds to answer each one of them prior to arriving at his conclusions which are definitive and absolute. "Animals, like us, have souls. ... . In a wonderful and unexpressionable way,... God is present in all creatures." *13

Listen to only a few of our well know visionaries and leaders. Listen to what Abraham Lincoln, Mark Twain, Thomas Edison, Leonardo DeVinci, Gandhi and Albert Schweitzer had to say about human relationships with animals.

~

"I am in favor of animal rights as well as human rights. That is the way of the whole human being." Abraham Lincoln.

~

"The greatness of a nation and its moral progress can be judged by the way its animals are treated." Gandhi

~

"I believe that I am not interested to know whether vivisection produces results that are profitable to the human race or doesn't. To know that the results are profitable to the race would not remove my hostility to it. The pain which it inflicts upon consenting animals is the basis of my enmity toward it, and it is to me sufficient justification of the enmity without looking further." Mark Twain

~

"Non-violence leads to the highest ethics, which is the goal of all evolution. Until we stop harming all other living beings, we are still savages." Thomas Edison.

~

"The day will come when men such as I will look upon the murder of animals the way they now look upon the murder of men." Leonardo De Vinci

~

"The man who has become a thinking being feels a compulsion to give will-to-live the same reverence that he gives his own. He experiences that other life in his own." Albert Schweitzer

14.

Sacred Trust

Animals are therapy for all of us. They don't judge but accept us without qualification despite our mistakes, limitations or successes. They are our healers, our guardians and our teachers. "Unselfish love" one therapist calls it. "Living examples of grace, honesty, trust and companionship," another says.

~

Thirty days after a dog, Dewey, dies his owner and companion rents a large scenic museum on the water's edge and throws a coat and tie, catered party for 150 friends celebrating the life of his dog. He invites his friends and the friends of Dewey. A large album of photographs of Dewey who loved all kids lies on the main table and quickly becomes the center of attention, laughter, joy and remembrance. Later when recalling the events of that one evening each person breaks into a sincere, boisterous laugh while joyfully exclaiming, "the finest and most joyful party I have ever attended."

15.

The Bluebirds

The year is 1981. By mid-April the fury of Mother Nature has already been fully spent. All winter long, violent twisting winds and heavy snowfalls pelts eastern US. In the apple country of central New England snow drifts to depths of over twelve feet high, covering both farmhouses and the connected barns, isolating families for weeks. But the wily farmer of the 1700 and 1800's who had drawn his livelihood from the soil and the weather for generations foresaw the crises of New England winters to both farmer and his livestock, and he had built his house and barn together as one unit, connected by a covered walkway. So neither man nor animal was any the worse off, despite the violence of the winter of 1981.

In one of the old farm houses close-by our old Farm Homestead in North central Massachusetts a middle aged couple is rejoicing at the departure of the last of the snow. After a rather long pause in their conversation, Marie, tall and silent, reads her husband's thoughts and says, "Doug, I know it is our tenth anniversary in a couple of days but please...no diamonds, and no jewelry."

She continues. "Honestly, honey, diamonds are cold and expensive, and they are useless to me. "Let's do something special for our tenth, something for our friends, the animals... something warm ... something personal ... something perhaps filled with life and the sense of renewal, just like the lovely Spring Seasons each year." Later that same evening they huddle and together they decide on an extraordinary gift for this very special Spring Season.

Perhaps, in her heart Marie already knew what she wanted, before she mysteriously read her husband's mind and shattered his hope of finally placing a diamond on her finger after a marriage of ten years. Or maybe something else inside stirred her to remember the open fields and orchards of their youths which were populated by the stunning Native American Eastern Bluebirds with peach colored breasts, and with backs and heads more striking than the brightest, clearest, cerulean, crystal sky. While watching the bluebirds years now past, she clearly recalls thinking, "they carry the magnificent bluest sky on their backs. Their hue of blue is as fresh as the hue of the clearest, sunny spring day, and their song is a celebration of love and of life." Often her father, himself, had said, "bluebirds are native here and ought to be America's National Bird."

"But the bluebirds that I remember are nearly extinct, now," she ponders to herself. "Hardly anyone below fifty years of age has even ever seen a bluebird. They are victims to other, more aggressive birds, the Starling and the English House Sparrow, both imported from Europe in the 1800s and who refused to share with the more passive bluebird the abandoned woodpecker nests and the cavities in the wooden fence post located in open fields. Human incursions also contributed to their demise, which also cost the bluebirds their nests in the boughs of apple trees. Since the trees were no longer productive they were simply cut down and used as firewood. Also wooden fence posts with knot holes were replaced with man hued iron posts. And the bluebird was no longer able to invite his mate to nest in the cavities there, and together to raise two or more broods each year."

Back at the old farmhouse in the apple country of central New England, now ten years after Marie had first shattered Doug's wish to give her a long over-due diamond ring for their tenth anniversary with the gentle but frank pronouncement, "No diamonds, and no jewelry," they are walking together through an open field near their farm, a field now bordered by a row of nesting boxes for bluebirds. There are ten nesting boxes in a row, each spaced two to three hundred feet apart. Doug has built the boxes himself and presented each one separately to his wife in the Spring, for the last ten consecutive years.

"My dream was to bring back the beautiful bluebirds to our farm," she quietly explains on this crisp, sunny morning. And now, ten years later I have my wish and my very own Bluebird Trail."

All morning long both husband and wife watch and marvel at the frenzy on the fences near the boxes and on the tops of the boxes themselves. Bright, crystal azure bluebirds who are brighter than the clear, fresh, spring morning are sitting there. Many males are warbling a yearning call to their chosen mates, imploring them to accept their invitations and their homes, and are popping in and out of the boxes. Other females have already accepted and are now building their nests inside the boxes while their mates extol their unrestrained joy in a rhapsody of passion, love and life. The frenzy continues all day long and later, as our couple returns to their old farmhouse each quietly hears another separate, higher pitch song, a song which blends with the bluebird mating sounds and the warbling. It too is a bluebird and a new resident. Together they stop and quietly listen for a long time to the chorus of crystal clear notes, notes which to them are a hymn of praise and gratitude from the bluebirds for the thoughtful and priceless work here of two very special human beings.

Part 111

Animal Tragedies

When the animals come to us, asking for our help, will we know what they are saying?

When the plants speak to us in their delicate beautiful language, will we be able to answer them?

When the planet herself sings to us in her dreams, will we be able to wake ourselves and act?

Gary Lawless

16.

Loss of Wonderment

While strolling along a path in the woods along the Potomac River two teenagers suddenly spy a large snapping turtle that has climbed out of the river, walked across a fifty yard strip of grass, tree roots, and a pathway, and is up on a highway in danger of being hit by an automobile. As fast as they could they dashed across the grass to the highway to capture her and place to her out of danger. But they are too late. Before they reach the concrete surface of the highway a car hits her, and they hear a faint scream from her that mixes with the thud from the tire, as the car continues on without slowing.

Together, brother and sister slowly carry her to a quiet place under a pine tree near the water and together sit beside her. Because of her large size they know that she is a female over forty years old who in mid-June is looking for a remote, soft, sandy nest to bury her eggs. Her shell is shattered and she is mortally wounded. Both teenagers talk to her and try to soothe her, and as they quietly watch she finally relaxes her tense neck and passes over into a calmer and perhaps gentler place.

~

Millions of wildlife are killed on American roadways every day, roadways which cross migration paths and forge deep into the hearts of animal habitats many centuries old, roadways which were constructed without considerations for wildlife. At the same time, other wildlife die in wetlands and marshes that are becoming dry or sour due to construction of drainage canals and blockages of streams, or are simply poisoned while grazing in fields or drinking water from brooks that are saturated with pesticides and herbicides.

~

A man trudges through shallow water and a marsh made stagnant by highway construction and housing development near Chicago to rescue a Canada Goose from botulism which has already claimed her mate. As he carries her away from the poisoned water she mystically places her strong neck on his shoulder and keeps it there until she is at the vet's clinic. But it is too late, try as they may to save her, it's too late.

~

Animals have always lived in harmony with the earth and with all the other creatures on the earth - taking only that which they needed to survive. The native people of America recognized this and closely observed the animals, learning from them and indeed putting into practice many of the lessons they learned through their observations.

For millenniums animals and humans lived in harmony before new civilizations evolved through conquest and un-kept promises. From new civilizations came the concept of Agriculture and the need for land that quickly turned to greed and the destruction of the older indigenous cultures.

17.

Maurice's Story

As a fifteen year old, while I was visiting my Grandfather's Farm in the apple country of New England I am told a story about my Grandfather's beautiful Shetland Ponies by Maurice, a neighbor and friend. For many months after, I am haunted by a succession of dreams of that story.

"Did your Grandfather ever tell you about that day with the ponies, the orchard and the poison,' Maurice asked. It was in early Spring, a year or two before you started coming here."

"No, I don't think that anyone ever mentioned that to me," I reply.

"I guess that he didn't want you to know. Perhaps, he thought you were too young, or maybe he just plain forgot."

Maurice hesitates, sips some cocoa, and then hesitates again. As I look at him he appears at first not to want to tell me, thinking perhaps that he made a mistake to bring it up. Sadness appears on his face, a deep, earthy, resigned sadness that appears to be reflecting his thoughts, like an old, sad movie film running through his head. He continues to stare at his old cup for a long time while running his fingers around the chipped edge.

He then starts talking. The tone of his voice is low and uncertain at first, but as he continues and is better able to picture the events of that one day his voice gets stronger and he speaks in a clear high pitched tone. He tells me a story that I have not heard before. When he finishes less than twenty minutes later neither one of us speaks. I don't think that either one of us could speak as a profound stillness settled over us, the deep peaceful stillness that seemed to come from the earth itself.

After a while we both went outside and he placed his small arm around me. My throat is very tight and I swallow hard remembering the story. Without another word passing between us, I left and slowly walked back to Gramp's old farmhouse. That night and for nearly the next month I vividly recalled Maurice's story in a succession of dreams, dreams that are to me vivid and real.

It's the beginning of Spring, and everything is just starting to turn green. The fields are very hilly and a weather-worn barn board fence with hand-split posts encloses two adjoining fields. There is a small pond at the lowest level in the center of the largest field. Up on the hills outside of the fences and extending as far as the eye could see there is a large apple orchard.

The pond used to be called the "Swamp" where nothing ever lived and no one ever ventured. "Your grandfather drained the land called the "swamp" which was filled with poisons that flowed from the insect and rodent sprays used in the nearby apple orchard. Once the pond had been cleaned of poisons that had flowed into it for years it was used as a watering pond for the ponies. It was used by ponies for the about five years," Maurice said.

There are two small, half grown Shetlands feeding high up in the south field, at the farthest point from the watering pond. I can see them standing there and grazing, occasionally throwing back their heads to look over the fence into the adjoining field. There are thirteen other ponies scattered throughout the large adjoining field, with the pond at the lowest level.

But something is wrong...very wrong. Except for the two half grown Shetlands in the south field who are separated from the others by a fence, none of the ponies are tossing their heads or even moving. In fact, the thirteen ponies are lying down on the ground motionless. Occasionally one moves with a sudden jerk, but just for a moment, and then everything is still again.

Suddenly, I'm aware of some movement among the ponies. A man is there, also. He is medium height and huskier than most men. I didn't see him at first because he is standing still beside the biggest of the ponies and his old worn out felt hat and his cloth coat blends in with the surroundings. His cloths and manner are familiar, and suddenly I recognize him.

It's Gramps! ... But Gramps seems much older, and his movements are much slower and seem tired this morning as he kneels beside his stallion, the sire of all the others except the oldest mares. He begins stroking the pony's neck and cleaning away white foam from the pony's mouth with a handkerchief he has drawn from his pocket. As he strokes, he bends farther over, closer to the pony's head and for a very long time he quietly talks into the ear of his prize Shetland. I want to run and help Gramps but I can't. I'm paralyzed and I can't move.

While I watch helplessly, Gramps reaches into his coat pocket, and just as I notice the sun reflecting on a metal object in his large hand, there is a pop, startling and alone, like the noise of a solitary limb from a tree cracking after an ice storm. The sick pony flinches and then stretches out and relaxes for the last time. Gramps remains there next to him and continues to talk to him, all the while stroking the ponies neck and wiping the deadly foam away from his mouth. Slowly Gramps moves to the next three largest ponies, his mares and repeats the ritual. Near the end of the morning, he is finished and slowly and painfully he moves toward the gate. The two half-grown ponies in the South field, the only two ponies alive now follow him to the gate. He holds the gate open so both can pass through into another field that is farther away from the poisoned ground water in the pond.

Unknown to Gramps or the Shetlands, the owner of the apple orchard in the Fall had placed arsenic around the tree's trunks to kill rodents and to prevent them from chewing bark off the tree trunks. Most of the poison settled on the surface of the earth and during the spring thaw the water around the trees that was saturated with arsenic washed into the small drinking pond, thereby poisoning the water. The poisoned water killed everything that drank there, including Gramps thirteen prized Shetland ponies.

Next, I remember what Maurice said when he told me the story. "That afternoon your Grandfather hired a back hoe and a driver. They dug a very deep, long trench and buried the thirteen ponies there. Your Grandfather didn't show up for the burial, I guess that he had said his good-byes earlier".

The Epilogue

Sometimes I wonder if humans originated somewhere else, on another planet perhaps and then simply happened on this planet by chance, for wherever we go and whatever we do we change everything on Planet Earth to suite us. We mutilate and wreck habitats and landscapes at the drop of a hat, regardless of the destruction to indigenous natives, ancient cultures, animals, climate, atmosphere, environment, in fact the whole living earth. And when irreplaceable, astonishing wildlife is in our path we simply exterminate the wildlife, not caring to look into the future, beyond ourselves while at the same time flouting the principle of *Reverence For All of Life* which is as old as humankind itself.

My best guess is that human beings did originate on earth and are not from another planet.

But the concept of humans originating from another planet has a point. During the last two centuries in particular, we have blatantly erased everything within our range. It is as if we feel compelled to change this world, or maybe we are simply taking her for granted or don't care, have given-up, or merely consider ourselves wanton occupants of a derelict property. On the other hand, perhaps we have been unsuspecting victims of our own imperfect languages and religions which for many, many generations may have restricted our thoughts and severely pruned them so that now they are deeply imbedded in a single, narrow line like a row of corn and our one-dimensional thoughts are attempting to cope in a multi-dimensional, vibrant, living world. Or perhaps we are simply confused, like a fledgling, and as a species we are not yet mature and are badly in need of direction and harmony.

For if to change our living planet to the detriment of everything else except ourselves be our quest, then we are in very grave danger. The living planet is our habitat and the summation of at least seventy million years of adaptation and survival. She is our oldest and wisest protector, our helmsman, pathfinder and our teacher. In fact, she is our very soul without which we will not exist. Without a nurturing, vibrant, living earth to guide and nourish us, we will simply vanish without a trace, like a cloud or a puff of smoke, and be gone forever.

In the vibrant future, ahead of us are many choices, all mixing together and we are all blindly groping our way toward our own enlightenment. The most extraordinary, inspirational, and refreshing of our travels are here on earth, wonders of the secrets of our living planet. For history is here in the making as it has always been, and our adventures are being recorded and we will be held accountable.

Future generations when tracking our passages will remember that ancient civilizations before us practiced cannibalism and considered slavery an inescapable presumption for all future civilizations and they will praise us for destroying the chains of human bondage and repression and replacing them with individual knowledge and enlightenment. However, they will also note with trepidation and dismay our enslavement, slaughter, and wanton destruction of our own living world, domestic animals, and wildlife, and they will wonder why we did not learn from our past blunders.

They will applaud our development and expansions of a whole range of meaningful sciences, but they most certainly will also ridicule our use of pesticides, fuels and chemicals which poison our people, our animals, our lands, our air, and our waters. And when they read of our tacit acceptance of destruction to habitat, to wildlife, and to the environment of our own planet, they will pause and question what we were thinking, or if we were even thinking anything at all. Fifty years ago, cancerous tumors in animals was almost unknown by veterinarians and animal caretakers, yet today, just over a decade and a half after the advent of the twenty first century, cancer which is almost certainly caused by a whole range of manufactured products and other by-products of human affluence including agricultural chemicals is found in an estimated 50% of domestic animals treated by veterinarians in the United States.

Most certainly future generations will approve of our efforts to enlarge the human experience and to extend the years of human life, but they will also know that a vegetarian's life exceeds by more than six years a meat eater's life, and they will be shocked by our addictions to a meat based diet. They will shake their heads in disbelief at the starvation on many continents and wonder if we knew that by cycling grain through humans directly rather than through animals there is 94% more food available to other humans. If North Americans alone reduced their consumption of meat by only ten percent, sixty million other people who are starving today will eat tomorrow. A meat eater in one year uses one acre yielding only 250 pounds of beef, yet that same single acre of land, if planted in vegetables yields a crop of up to 70,000 pounds of vegetables. And to produce one kilogram of meat takes 16 times more labor and 7 times more fossil fuel than to produce one kilogram of grain protein.

While marveling at our climate controlled robotics industries and praising us for our personal understanding of some of our domestic animals, they will openly condemn the farm animal factories with their massive filthy animal confinement prisons and slaughterhouses as vacuous, savage, cannibalistic and non-caring, and the hunting and trapping of defenseless, astonishing wildlife for sport or for any other reason as barbaric, blinded and cruel.

The story of our advancements in some health sciences will be praised and cherished, but future generations will also most certainly retch and sicken at the animal science laboratories. Alternative solutions in place of animal torture and destruction which are routinely practiced in the more enlightened scientific laboratories are always superior, far more visionary and cheaper, and do not numb our own senses nor wreak havoc upon the intricate web of life within our own planet. When we finally realize and openly vocalize that harming animals in any way and for any purpose is not an alternative, scientific laboratories will find other innovative and better solutions.

"Teachers, what did you teach?

Scientists! What did you learn and understand?

Healers! What did you heal?

Ministers of the church! What did you preach," future generations will ask.

Children of the Earth! Where were you? Why did you not fight for our living world? Did not your parents, relatives and friends take you for walks through woods so that you may learn the awe and wonders of this planet and so that in future decades of your lives you may return to the woods, fields and meadows for personal nourishment and refreshment.

For what does it matter if we destroy Mother Earth in one solitary catastrophic explosion or one piece at a time, what is lost is lost forever, and we are forever diminished.

Perhaps we only need time to grow in order to come full circle, to the point where all humans display unmitigated love and compassion, and absolute respect and awe for the wonder of animals and our vibrant living planet. But our self-destruction is outpacing our understanding and our healing, and the devastation to animals, habitat and all the living planet continues to accelerate at a horrifying pace. What will we answer future generations when they ask these same questions, if future generations will even continue to exist at all?

Albert Einstein, who scratched the surface of the unraveling of humankind's deep and dependent interactions to the universe through mathematics spoke of our responsibilities and relationships with all living beings and Planet Earth in this way. "(A human being) experiences himself, his thoughts, and feelings as something separate from the rest -- a kind of optical delusion of his consciousness. This delusion is a kind of prison for us, restricting us to our personnel desires and to affection for a few persons nearest to us. Our task must be to free ourselves from this prison by widening this circle of compassion to embrace all living creatures and the whole of nature in its beauty."*23

The End

"I was sad one day and went for a walk;
I sat in a field.
A rabbit noticed my conditioned and came near,
To just be close to creatures who
Are so full of knowing,
So full of love and they don't chat,
They just gaze with their marvelous
*understanding."*9*

Acknowledgements

The research for *Talking for Animals* has been life-long and extensive. To the many authors, editors, poets and publishers that I have referenced I tender my gratitude. If I have omitted anyone I apologize and if notified I will make corrections in future editions. Also, I am indebted to friends who contributed, to my late parents who allowed this kid free range on the farm and woods, and both of my brothers who grew up with me as we learned to joyfully respect this miraculous place.

Roger Ethier is former *Technical Adviser* for the UN for Sustainable Technologies and Agriculture and has travelled throughout the planet while working in over 20 countries. He is also founder of *Engineers without Borders International.*

Vibrant human relationships to people, animals and nature dominate many of the short stories he has authored for national and international publications including a story featured in all national and international editions of Readers Digest. His work has been translated into French and Russian and was especially selected by US Librarians to be placed on CDs for the physically challenged blind.

Bibliography

1. Anderson, Lorraine Sisters of the Earth, (1991) Vintage, New York

2. Barber, T.X. The Human Nature of Birds, (1993) St Martins' Press, New York

3. Berril, N.J. The Life of the Ocean, (1966) McGraw, New York

4. Berril, N.J. Journey into Wonder, ((1953) Dodd, Meade, New York

5. Berril, N.J. Man's Emerging Mind, (1955) Faucett, Greenwich, Conn.

6. Beston, Henry, The Outermost House, (1988) Penguin Books, New York

7. Burroughs, John, John Burroughs' America (1951) Devin-Adair, Greenwich, Conn

8. Caras, Roger, Animals in their Places, (1987) Sierra Club Books, San Francisco, Ca.

9. Dyer, Wayne W., Change Your Thoughts-Change Your Life, (2007) Hay House Inc., NYC

10. Ethier, Roger, Chesapeake Bay GoosemusiC, (1996) Folklore Press, Alexandria, VA

11. Ethier, Roger, Happiest Place on Earth, (1997) Folklore Press, Alexandria, VA

12. Fox, Michael W. Inhumane Society, (1990) St Martin's Press, NYC, NY

13. Fox, Michael W., Boundless Circle, (1996) The Theosophical House, Wheaton, Il

14. Kowalski, Gary A. The Souls of Animals, (1991) Stillpoint Publishing, Walpole, NH

15. Lorenz, Konrad, The Year of the Graylag Goose, (1979) Harcourt Brace Jonanovich, NYC, NY

16. Masson, J. Moussaieff When Elephants Weep, Delacorte, NYC, NY

17. McElroy, Susan Chernak, Animals as Teachers and Healers, (1996) New Sage press, Troutman, OR.

18. Robbins, John, May All Be Fed, (1992) W. Morrow, New York

19. Roberts, Elizabeth and Amidon, Elias, Earth Prayers (1991).

20. Roberts, Elizabeth and Amidon, Elias, Life Prayers (1996).

21. Roberts, Monty, The Man Who Listens to Horses, (1997) Random House, New York

22. Ryden, Hope, God's Dog (1979) Lyons and Burford, New York.

23. Schweitzer, Albert, Reverence for Life, (1969) Harper, New York

24. Tobias, Michael, Cowen, Georgianne, edited by, The Soul of Nature, (1996) Plume, New York

25. Willoya, Warriors of the Rainbow, (1962) Naturegraph, Happy Park Ca

26. Wynne-Tyson, Extended Circle, (1985) Paragon House, New York

27. Zelney, Lawrence, The Bluebirds, (1976) Indiana University Press, Bloomington, IN